SAILOR'S BLUE

I0079094

Kayleigh Campbell has a Ph.D in Creative Writing and currently teaches in Higher Education. Her work has appeared in the likes of *Butcher's Dog Magazine*, *The Rialto* and *The North Magazine*. She has previously been commended for Troubadour International Poetry Competition and shortlisted for the Bridport Prize in Poetry. She currently lives in North Yorkshire with her partner and two children.

Also by Kayleigh Campbell

Notes on Different Places   (Salò Press, 2024)

Matryoshka   (Verve Poetry Press, 2022)

Keepsake   (Maytree Press, 2019)

CONTENTS

ISBN: 978-1-916938-89-2

The author has asserted their right to be identified as the author of this Work in accordance with the Copyright, Designs and Patents Act 1988

Cover designed by Aaron Kent

Edited by Stuart McPherson

Typeset by Aaron Kent

Broken Sleep Books Ltd
PO BOX 102
Llandysul
SA44 9BG

Sailor's Blue

Kayleigh Campbell

Broken Sleep Books

JULY

Good lighting as an antidepressant,
unidentified purple flowers. A man
with a hollow head, a fox inside the moon.
Dogs as academics. Food stuck in teeth.
Ice cream melting down hands. Translations,
correct or not. A ceiling made of lanterns,
a wall of keyboards. Two black cats, parallel.
Bodies drying like towels in the sun.
Women in pink cubes, neon. A wolf looking
down on us. Sleeping on the floor, after sun.
I love you written on an apartment building,
twice, anon. Stuffed animals using exercise
equipment. Wild flowers in a wine bottle.
Tramlines, sweat marks, a pygmy hippo.
One sip of Mango Lassi. Heat, quiet.
Lime green train seats, reflections in
the window, crossing borders.

MOTHER WAVE
After Roseanne Watt

i've searched since birth
ready to plunge into
the undercurrent
that might take me
somewhere like home

BORDERLANDS

I'm wearing a summer dress
it is a light shade of green
think sea foam or pistachio
it's like I am playing a game
a balloon under my dress
soon to be replaced with a doll
whose eyes are not always open
we are driving back from some
farm / play area / gift shop
early summer
my daughter is in the back
pinafore no tights
hair in a sweaty bun
finishing an ice lolly
I know my way back enough
forgo the sat nav so she can
watch YouTube kids
the car is a greenhouse now
my cheeks something like tomatoes
I can hear some video playing
I can feel limbs moving under my dress
under my skin
my eyelids start to close
I fight them blink / blink / blink
take a sip of water
but they try again
then I am in a land of light
there is nobody else

only sunflowers and small white bugs flying
I go to lay down in the field
and then the rumble strip
jolts me back over

SEPTEMBER

A red velvet bedframe
lonely, roadside. A worm
rolled in sand, sliced in two.
Temporarily unavailable car.
Small bodies wrapped in white
sheets, homes on fire. A woman
refusing to make herself anonymous.
A hug from a stranger, no longer
strange. Half a tangerine as a
thank you. A child learning
the word beautiful. Marshmallow
sky. Rain splattered on the window,
a small packet of gummy bears.
A desk chair lonely, roadside.

CHANGELING

my daughter tells us of her old family
from a hundred years ago   [the time can change]
of her closest friend   a girl named Keedie
[her age can change]   [location can change]
she describes to us how she   plucked
soft blossom petals   in Kyoto
lived in an apartment block   in Bucharest
was commander of a ship   in the North Sea
queen of a forest   in Denmark
that Keedie keeps her awake   sometimes
i see her often staring into   some kind of space
wonder where she's looking   if it is something
like i saw once   sometimes still do

SAILOR'S BLUE
After Seabear

the weather report is insignificant
early hours are not unavailable
my body aches
i eventually slip

i touch the sea beneath my boat
my hands are already cold
it feels like a lukewarm bath

i've made a sail from your jumper
i'm heading towards the ghost town
to look for you
all I have is my boat the sea
a map of your face

PAUL MESCAL

It comes to me when I'm unpacking,
moving our crumpled pyjamas to the wash bin,
putting the toiletry bag which matches
the overnight bag back in the bathroom,
that I'm Paul Mescal when he was
a sun-satined dad.

I check my face in the mirror.
I still look like me. I'm not a dad
and I'm not playing anything.
I sit down on the bed holding
your heart print top.

When you remember our trips
together, I think you'll see pancakes
with edible flowers, chaos and Frankenstein
in the Young V & A. The name of our
tube stop. Making up our own language.

You probably will, but your memory
might also display me in a vivid-cool filter
not smiling with my eyes half-playing
your game amongst rows of old clocks.

You might picture me looking
past you in the Thai restaurant,
hear me asking if you're having
a good time.

You might remember us there, but
know now that I was somewhere else too.

CAPTAIN

the sea is hungover
thrashing and retching
a shade of post-party blue
the rain comes
insolent and heavy
prodding the sea
an orca breaches
a gleam in its eye
a wide conical smile
the boat shudders
something bangs
against the side
she buttons her coat

SHADOW

My daughter eyes the bloodied tissue
asks when she will get hers
when you're older I say
she bounds back into the room

I look at myself in the mirror
place my fingertips on her
fingermarks on the wall
made with my lipstick

OCTOBER

It was late in the month
and thick with dry heat.
Pleasure and concern
mixed together with sweat.

We did bask in it, but
knew it was warning us.
Then the ladybirds came,
hundreds of them covering
the back of our house,
creeping into it.

PATELLIFORM

When you were little,
you could turn into a limpet.
You were wild like sails
on a blustery autumn day,
then suddenly rigid clinging
to my thigh.

Gently, I'd rub your back
you'd soften, run your little
hands over and over
the bottom of my dress
before gripping the fabric
curling your fingers,
your cheek to my thigh.
I have limpet
marks up my leg, like height
marks on a wall.

LIMINAL

ten pm / mid-july / clement /she's walking the border/
Charlottenburg & Wilmersdorf district / alone / not alone /
she is passed by men in leather / normal people / street after
street / walking / somewhere / crossings / neon lights /
nollendorfplatz / she passes herself from years before / doorways
illuminated numbers / the hotel entrance / dreaming

SURFACING

1.

I am surrounded by oak
and maple, lose my footing
on the rugged ground.
I do not know this place
                      understand
that it does not know me.

It is pacific; goosebumps rise
my skin a plucked bird.
There is a ghostliness here,
things watching me from
behind tree trunks.
My hands have small cuts,
as do my shins and calves.
My blood is sap: drying,
hardening then glistening
on the rocks.

A gust of wind flicks at my face,
sharp and startling.
I feel the sense to move,
like that first urge to push.
I follow the sounds of the sea.

2.

I am on the beach now,
a metre away from the restless
taunting water. I did not feel
unwanted by the trees, only
that they were ushering me here.

Now I am facing it, I want to turn
back into the shade and solace
of the forest. I have seen the sea
over and over, the different faces of it.

But never here; I am the oldest
I have been and the most uncertain.
I edge backwards. Then an anchor,
a hand on my shoulder.
A gathering around me.

3.

They don't speak but motion for
me to follow them into the boat,
I move away from the shore.
They speak openly, I can't understand
but do not feel like an outsider;
their small smiles I can decipher.

After some time we stop, they mark
their spot. They begin their descent
quickly, together over the edge,
fins saluting me as they dive under.
One of the women stays with me,
offers me the tools I need, places
her hand on mine and nods, gently.

I forget to spit; everything turns to cloud.
The sea woman takes it from me,
clears my vision, advises me with
movements of hands and head.
We go in together.

4.

At first it is only darkness, a room
with no light or gaps. I feel the panic
hurtling through my chest up into
my throat but I force myself to focus.
I see them then, the sea women below
me, some making their way upwards
again. The woman who helped me
made her descent like a swift.

I hover, suspended in sea and time.
I won't last much longer, though
the haenyeo knew I wouldn't.
They just knew I needed to do
the hard part.
I breach the surface.

GARLAND

what is a birthday
without one
pastel-coloured
joy   in paper form
left up for days   afterwards
to ease us back
to make the coming week
less ordinary

today we made a garland
a nonsensical note
a postcard from Belgium
a wilted dandelion
a restaurant receipt
a newborn crochet hat
a tissue-paper moon
a lifeless moth
a day in April

leave it hanging
for the rest of the year

REFUGE
After Melodie Stacey

she made her way to a forest
no directions or supplies
she kept looking behind
stumbling on fallen branches
until she found the heart

she looked to the waning moon
listened for the sound of feet
crushing leaves then climbed
kept climbing until almost
at the top spread out her limbs
her hair turned to pine

ADAPTING

We sank into the fabric of the sofa,
the way weetabix slowly submerges
into milk. We sat in the quiet
as though it was a hammock gently
rocking, wanting to talk about our
day but knowing the needs of that
moment. After sitting, browsing small
screens we turned on the TV.
Pause: we heard the familiar sound
of something banging. I brought the little
tired, wired boy back downstairs.
He ran around, emptied baskets we'd just
tidied. Not long after we heard the considered
footsteps of his sister, not one to miss
out on an opportunity. We put Bluey on,
sat together again as we did only
some hours earlier.

FUNAYŪREI

In a small sailboat
she begins the journey
across the ocean,
a cloudless night,
a moonless night;
the moon is now an onigiri
in her pocket, ready to throw
to the ghosts beneath her.

THE BODY KNOWS

At first she thought it was normal, that it must've
been raining heavily before she left the house.
The water covered the road, level with the curb.
When she needed to cross she had no choice
but to step into it, her canvas shoes soaking
like a sponge. Others did not seem to notice.
When she reached the office she noticed dripping
from the ceiling, figured there must be a leak.
She was responding to emails when she realised
the room was filling with water. She became still
like a rock; the frigid water seeping through
her clothes. She gasped. Her office was basement
level, she looked out to the carpark that was now
underwater, the water now prising its way in
through the windows. She waded out of her office
her heart racing. She alerted those around her,
only to be met with blank expressions and dry clothes.

KINTSUGI

she can't remember the day that it was
when her body cracked into pieces

but she remembers the daffodils
the crocuses gathering on the grass

as she picked herself up bound the pieces
back together with gold

PLAY

My daughter asks if we can play
orca shows again. Another heirloom:
two orcas, one more realistic,
an elephant, rhino, blue whale,
hippo, two reindeer, a crocodile.
A lion who chased her father
through Beaumont Park, it's
perpetual snarl, manic eyes.
Tonight I am a barbie, no clothes
but some shoes. My daughter
is the orca, the realistic one,
and she performs as I watch.
As always, she instructs me
on what to do, what to say.
I can feed fish to the orca,
then I can dive with the orca;
the orca likes my hair. I break
character and look at her,
but she carries on. She is five
and can't know the reference.

NOVEMBER

A swallowed tooth, a hedgehog torn to pieces,
a field of lavender. Cold coffee and socks
on the stairs, a crash on the slip road.
Neon pastries, sliced grapefruit, green juice
with too much lemon in, a party straw.
A child staring into space, flanked by disheveled
parents outside a city centre Wetherspoons.
A wall full of post it notes. Glass jars full
of chocolate drops, a glass jar full of
umbilical stump. Grace Darling's grave.
Yin and yang cats, a dead baby bird
by the front door, a half-built Wendy house.
A fixed gutter, the sound of rain at night.
Unexpected warm days in September,
crying at Paul Mescal dancing, poppies
growing out of concrete, sand in the bottom
of bags. Hearing the cat come in,
waking up then going back to sleep.

I HOPE YOU ARE WELL?

there is a beeping
like the one when someone
has forgotten their seatbelt
or when the fridge has been
left open for too long
or the fire alarm batteries need
replacing and every minute or
two it bleeps asking for help
i can hear the beeping
but i don't know where it is
coming from or what it means

ALMOST

after Margarita García Robayo

she learned that families
are flammable places
how close we lay with
violence the temptation to be cruel
to push through boundaries
like breaking the surface of water
when she was just a young girl
her brother too a young
boy nearly drowning her
because she stole his rubber
shape filled with air

CELESTE

she turned off the lights
walked to the top of the house
stopping outside a door
she put on her silk dressing gown
opened the door
stepped out into nothingness
a strangely comforting darkness
she hopped from luminous point to point
then dived into the sea of space
hurtling back towards earth
as a shooting star

THE VILLAGE

There are daffodils lining the long
winding road, some are without their heads.

We pass a house which looks like it should be in Fargo.
Inside sits a matriarch with a gun, money and bones
hidden in the walls.

There is always someone walking their dog.
They smile, their silent rage and secrets
teetering behind the tight but pleasant hello.

All the seasons exist together here.
Deer roam in the field next to the park.

Children watch us from behind sticky glass.
There is little noise in the daytime, but we know
things are moving, inside houses, underground.

You can hear the owls at night, their ominous calls.
The cooling towers watch over us, rising steam
like mushroom clouds. The trees stand guard.

We moved our things box by box, settled into
the village where we remain strangers.

HOW TO MAKE FLOWERS LAST

she once read that fairy lights
can make even a dead body look nice
flowers are like that too
the world is decaying
but a newly planted flower box
makes everything better
she took a daisy to a tattooist
now she always has at least
one flower to distract her
from the all the decomposition

PYJAMAS

she doesn't know what they looked like

if they had a pattern on them
if they were colourful
if they were too tight
if they were loose fitting
if they were a favourite pair

but she couldn't stop thinking of them
not *them,* but the small boy
curled up by his cold father,
both already gone

she can't stop thinking of
children under rubble,
pyjamas covered in dust and blood,
burnt polyester

she can't stop thinking of children
who've never felt the comfort
of soft, patterned cotton

she always liked the word *pyjamas*
but now when she hears it, or when
she picks up her son's small top and trousers
from the bedroom floor,
the lump comes back

she takes her son's pyjamas, folds them
neatly, holds them to her chest
and lays them down on the pillow,
gently

RABBIT

I try to keep big, bad things from them.
Death and violence, ignorance.

I tell my daughter not to watch scary videos,
make her promise to watch nice things.

I let them nearly flood the bathroom
because they find it funny, makes them happy.

After school one Tuesday, in a season I forget,
next door's cat walks along the fence with a baby

rabbit in its mouth, already dead, floppy ironically.
Omg, that's so crazy, my daughter says,

half smiling,
                amazed.

BARCELONA

eventide
the sky is palma violet
the sand is covered in bodies
breathing
some kind of living
the sea is giddy now
a mother and daughter
play with it
let themselves be lifted
the sea is zealous
wraps them into a tight
embrace
engulfing
some of the bodies
on the sand sit to
make a right angle
survey the scene
as the mother pulls
the daughter onto
the sand which covers
them like a blanket
the daughter cries
the mother cradles
they breathe in out
as does the sea
a few minutes pass
the daughter stands
ready to play again

CLAY

we begin the worksop with a flesh-like mound
are given tools wood and wire shells and hessian
we are told we can drag or smooth pierce or press
we can pull it apart examine the fibres
we set to work smoothing then piercing sculpting
what we might've been had we made ourselves

DELIVERY

It started in the cinema.
Paddy Considine was suffering
the repercussions of a head trauma.
His baby was crying so he picked
it up, took it into the utility room,
shut the door. A rush of hormones
burst from my body as ugly sobs.
I went to the toilet to recover.
The back pain started on the bus,
contractions all through the night.

Actual labour was quick enough,
a bloodied small pop like bubblegum
then pushing burning, retching.
She was small, no tears, one final push.
She cried immediately, but was not placed
in another room, instead handed to me
for skin to skin. The midwives praised me
all smiles, that I couldn't match.
I handed her to her dad, her soft skin
on his goosebump-bare chest.
I stood for the first time in 3 hours.
A clot of blood fell from me
like a big blob of paint. It was dark,
like a black hole. I wanted to jump
into it.

WORMS CAN FEEL PAIN, RESEARCH INDICATES

My daughter points to a worm
on the pavement and says

it's dead!

She says this because it is cut in three,
jelly-like, flattened.

I hurry her along when I see
the worm is still moving.

She knows death already,
but not yet suffering.

THINGS SEEN, HEARD AND DONE ON BUSES

- A women high on drugs slapped her in the face
- News of a suicide
- Gridlock
- News of an attempted suicide
- Anger at student letting companies
- A small boy face down on the beach, on the front of a tabloid
- Trying to cry quietly

FORGET ME NOT
After Joy Alpuerto Ritter

Everything has been laced
in darkness, save for one beam
of light, its base a glowing
circle. The girls walks into
the middle of it and she feels
like the centre of the universe.
She begins to cry, tears
of everything. Her hands
are now clutching flowers,
a bouquet for all occasions.
The violins start playing,
the bow sending vibrations
across the strings and her bones.
She too, has the gift of being
truly blue.

SLOW

I once read that we should learn
to be patient, to sit comfortably
in waiting rooms. I've stopped
skipping adverts, started browsing every
supermarket aisle. I drive at the speed
or just below the limit, started eating
and drinking slower. I've been letting
my hair dry naturally, been laying flat
on my stomach every time I come across
a snail, matching its pace, shifting my body
so slightly while leaving an aimless silvery trail.

DRIFTING

studies suggest that people
prefer showers to baths
something about not wanting
to bathe in your own filth
something about standing up
underneath warm rain
it is true there is no comparison
for cleanliness
for environmentally-friendliness
for efficiency
but there is something about
almost floating
closing your eyes listening
to the sounds of the open ocean

INTIMACY

i knew you would be good for me
when i set your toiletry basket on fire

and you were quietly alarmed
but helped me extinguish it

said it was a bit of excitement for the evening
we used the same melted basket

for another year

SEA GIRL

Her name was never known,
or her story.

It is known that she suffered
in her short life.

Thrown into the water
like a stone, or a plastic bottle

as if she were an object
of no value.

Washed up on the sand,
unknown and unwanted.

But we will call her sea girl,
and when the sand huddles

between our toes, when the
tide rushes over our feet

we can remember her,
love her, somehow, from ashore.

INDISTINCT CHATTER IN A DISTANT HALLWAY

it was somewhere around 11pm
the lights were still on
she just wanted them
to turn the fucking lights out
the middle ward
a holding pen
to make sure she was feeding
before they let her out
she just wanted to go home
but when she got home
she didn't know just how much
she'd feel homesick

GULLFOSS

if our children ask me what love really is
i'll show them our less tired faces
red from whippings of Icelandic wind
i'll tell them about your commitment
to saving me like Sigridur fought
for her falls

THE ART OF NOT GETTING MAD AT PEOPLE WHO DON'T DESERVE IT

Your son is ten months old
your daughter is four,
you are sat on a plane waiting to take off.
Your son is drifting asleep, you smile
at each other, perfect timing;
he is what angels actually look like.
A member of cabin crew walks by,
busily preparing for departure,
drops a payment device on his head.
He erupts into sobbing.
She apologises, apologises, apologises.
You are speechless, devastated.
You take a long,   deeeeeeeeep breath,
and say,
it is ok, not their fault.
You accept a free tea and coffee,
and everyone begins the journey.

QUESTIONS FROM KIDS

My friend's mother used to be a midwife.
I was at their house for tea,
chicken nuggets, beans and smiley faces,
when I suddenly asked if she'd ever
delivered a stillborn.

Yes, she replied bluntly, bemused.
I asked if she was sad, if it happens a lot.
Yes it made me sad, she said,
but you get used it.

DAGGER

A sailor inks a swallow
onto their skin for every
five thousand nautical miles.
Sailing around the world
would earn you approximately
four point one six swallows.
For those lost at sea, a dagger
through a swallow heart.
She has swallows on her chest,
arms and legs, each pierced
with a dagger, for all the years
she has lost.

DECEMBER
after girl in red

If we smoked we might have been smoking
cigarettes on the roof.

If I had more in my stomach than a cereal bar,
a mostly-rum mojito, some raki, archers and lemonade

I might've been able to appreciate the moon-lit
neon-glazed, winter city view.

I might have heard you say *don't look down*
because you won't be needing that route.

ABERYSTWYTH

Navy blue sea-front terrace
Houseplants
You named them all
I wanted to be a plant
Waxy deep Sacramento green
Centre of your windowsill
My face glistened like dewy foliage
I drove home in the rental car
The smell of you in my suitcase
A small succulent in the passenger seat

BOX

I carry it with me, made of glass
with things inside: fragile things
wrapped in tissue paper.

My daughter wants to know
what's inside, then gets distracted
asking if she can use it to make
a mini aquarium.

I say one day I will empty it,
we will fill in with sea water,
anemone and baby jellyfish.

HALCYON

The waves have been out sculpting again,
our feet cross their ridges in the sand.
It is not yet summer but the evening
sun is mellowed, reflecting off milk teeth,
a zebra jumper. We collect shells in our
hands, sand underneath our fingernails.
The clouds are low and grey, but not
unwelcome, they hover over us like
windbreakers, leaving gaps for the light.
The playground is all concrete, primary
colours, graffiti; the gate is fish skeleton.
It feels like the earth's end, and the start
of it. It feels something like home.

ABSCHIED

Alphabet floor, miscommunication.
Old runways for recreational use,
walking but moving nowhere. Kiwi,
how do you want it slicing?
Cabbage white butterflies, blocked paths,
the shade under trees. You make me love.
Flies landing on skin, loveable garlic.
Buildings in sunglasses, smoking cats,
unwanted housekeeping. Do you love life?
Wind turning the page, new shoe blisters
or just inadequate socks. Tiny spiders
on arms, blades of grass imprinted on thighs.
Angry man on a bike, riding with one hand,
asking why is it so complicated?
Fabric rainbows, fake plants in stairways.
Mice on metro tracks, heads on sticks.
A goodbye.

ACKNOWLEDGEMENTS

For Joe, Eliza & Alex, always.

'Play' was long listed in *The London Magazine* Poetry Prize 2024

An alternative version of 'Intimacy' appeared in *The North Magazine* Issue 69 (2023)

LAY OUT YOUR UNREST